IT's SIMPLE, HE HAS
To change in aro
ME To feel hap
I feel much better now that
I've given up hope.

For you alone,
from
yours appreciatively,
Ashleigh
Brilliant

Note: The above is guaranteed to be a genuine facsimile of my autograph.

(See inside) A.B.

Appreciate Me Now and Avoid the Rush©

Yet More Brilliant Thoughts
by
Ashleigh Brilliant

Creator of Pot-Shots®

and author of

I May Not Be Totally Perfect,
but Parts of Me Are Excellent©

and

I Have Abandoned My Search for Truth
and Am Now Looking for a Good Fantasy©

Published by
Woodbridge Press Publishing Company
Santa Barbara, California 93111

Published by

Woodbridge Press Publishing Company
Post Office Box 6189
Santa Barbara, California 93111

Published simultaneously in the United States and Canada

Printed in the United States of America

Library of Congress Cataloging in Publication Data

Brilliant, Ashleigh, 1933-
  Appreciate me now, and avoid the rush.

  1. Epigrams. 2. American wit and humor, pictorial. I. Title.
PN6281.B66   818′.5402   81-11582
ISBN 0-912800-97-6   AACR2
ISBN 0-912800-94-1 (pbk.)

Dedication

*This book would have been dedicated
to all the teachers
who have inspired and encouraged me —
if any of them
ever had.*

In This Book...

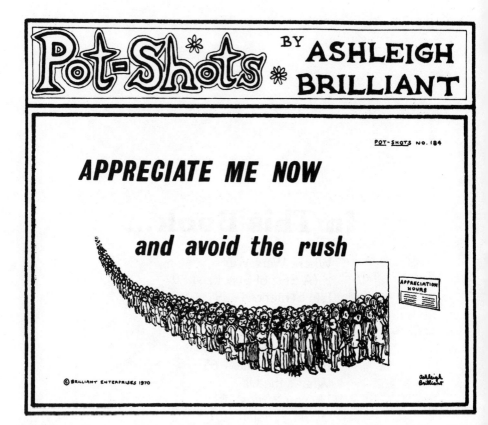

Where Were We?

(A Sort of Synopsis)

What! Another book of original, illustrated Brilliant Thoughts? Yes — my third in three years. And if you are wondering how this could have happened, be assured that it amazes me too. Not that I ever doubted my ability to do some very special things with words and images. But I never expected to encounter such a demand for repeat performances. On the other hand, there are still a few billion people in the world who are only beginning to become aware of my existence. If you happen to be one of these, let me explain a few basic things:

These messages, also called *Pot-Shots*, were originally published as separate postcards, which I still consider the ideal medium for them. None is longer than seventeen words (an arbitrary decision, made at the outset). They are intended as a universal aid to communication, and have been written with easy translation very much in mind. They now appear in many different forms, including newspaper syndication, and on a variety of licensed products (often with different art, but always, if legitimate, with the name Ashleigh Brilliant, which really has been my name since birth). They are individually copyrighted, and the copyright has been sustained in U.S. Federal Court. A Catalogue of my postcards and other items is available (see end of the book for details).

In an attempt to resemble more traditional literary works, this collection, like its predecessors, is divided into twelve chapters, each with a short preamble purporting to set a particular theme. But you incur no penalty for ignoring this subterfuge, and, by dipping in at random, you can effectively reconstruct the original disorder of my mind.

Who Was I?

For students of my life, the following facts may be of some interest:

1933 Born in London, England, 100 years after the birth of the founder of the Nobel Prize for Literature, and exactly 100 years before the celebration of my own Centenary.

1939 By accompanying my mother on what unexpectedly becomes a two-year visit to her home town of Toronto, Canada, my sister and I somehow bring on the Second World War.

1941- Life as a little wartime expatriate in Washington D.C.,
1946 where my father was a civilian member of the British Admiralty Delegation.

1947- Residing with my parents and sister on the outskirts of
1952 London in Edgware, attending (what was then called) Hendon County School, studying for endless examinations, and escaping from it all whenever possible on long hitchhiking trips.

1952- As a student of history at University College, London, I
1955 learn how to have a modern nervous breakdown.

1957 After emigrating to California, I train and qualify as a public high school teacher at Claremont Graduate School, only to commit the brief folly of actually taking employment in that capacity at Hollywood High School.

1958- In San Jose, California, I learn to fly, then enroll in Russian
1959 studies at the local state college, where I accidentally lose
my heart to a fellow student. We travel to Russia together.

1960- At the University of California at Berkeley, I acquire
1964 plentiful material for lifelong nightmares about academic
failure, but emerge with a prized and despised Ph.D. in
American History. Somewhere along the way, my lost
heart is returned to me.

1965 After failing in efforts to bring civilization and enlight-
enment to the town of Bend, Oregon, I find salvation at
last on board a "floating university," teaching history and
geography while sailing twice around the world.

1967 In San Francisco, I practise public self-therapy as an open-
air speaker in Golden Gate Park, and begin to publish my
Thoughts as postcards.

1968- I am espoused by Dorothy Tucker, a former fellow
1971 teacher, and forced into open pseudorespectability as a
businessperson. Our honeymoon is short but exciting
(two hours on the Farallon Islands, courtesy of the U.S.
Coast Guard, who thought we were doing research).

1973 Despite my yearning to become an underground hero,
Dorothy never lets my project get under the ground.
Returning from two years of world travels, we establish
ourselves in her ancestral home of Santa Barbara,
California, where this chronicle now abruptly terminates,
since it is against the law for anything of real importance to
happen in Santa Barbara.

Success (More or Less)

As a keen observer of my own career, I am often baffled as
to how to assess whatever it is that I have so far achieved. And
society at large seems to be having just as much difficulty in
evaluating and rewarding me. Financially, I am not yet a
millionaire, and not even remotely close to being one. But I
don't go hungry, and I do go occasionally on expensive trips to
places like Australia, China, and Antarctica. Alluring women
do not yet throw themselves at my feet in large numbers, or
even in small numbers. But I do, now and then, receive

I ALWAYS LIKE TO KNOW WHAT I'M DOING,

Ashleigh Brilliant

BUT THERE ARE TIMES

WHEN NOBODY WILL TELL ME.

© ASHLEIGH BRILLIANT 1979.

What I like most about myself is that I'm so understanding when I do something wrong.

Ashleigh Brilliant

© BRILLIANT ENTERPRISES 1977

invitations to appear in person, together with my wisdom, before groups of curious people, sometimes even at their own expense. The committees who award prestigious national and international literary prizes all seem to be holding back in confusion, secretly daring each other to be the first to honor me. But I do receive all kinds of verbal praise — much from strangers, some from friends, and once or twice even from my own family. I am continually being assured that my work is of value, and (somewhat less frequently) that, as its creator, I myself must somehow also be of some value.

And every once in a while something extraordinary does happen to make me feel really successful. Once, for example, shortly after my first book came out, I met a young man and woman who showed me that they had a copy of it, and that it was in rather battered condition. They explained that, over a period of several days, she had been paying more attention to my book than to him, and that he had finally expressed his frustration by throwing it at her. Now surely, *that* is some kind of success!

But it's not only as a missile that my work can prove itself. In fact, although it hasn't happened yet, I am looking forward to the day when somebody tells how a book of mine, or perhaps a pack of my postcards, actually saved a life —possibly by stopping a bullet. If nothing else, that would nicely demonstrate the value of these Thoughts as a kind of protective armor.

In the meantime, however, I must take what consolation I can in more modest glories, such as that of being associated with names of already established eminence. For example, in its February, 1980, edition, the *Reader's Digest* chose to print one of my Thoughts immediately following a (very sensational) article about Edward Kennedy (p. 242). It was Brilliant Thought No. 398: *ALL I ASK IS A CHANCE TO PROVE THAT MONEY CAN'T MAKE ME HAPPY*. Then, just four months later, the same magazine put me for the first time on its regular page of "Quotable Quotes," and I found myself rubbing literary shoulders with the likes of Goethe, H.G. Wells, Francis Bacon, and Seneca — all for having simply said: *EVERY TIME I CLOSE THE DOOR ON REALITY, IT COMES IN THROUGH THE WINDOW*. (Brilliant Thought No. 586; *Reader's Digest*, June,

Ashleigh
Brilliant

IT'S STRANGE, BUT
    WHEREVER I TAKE MY EYES,
        THEY ALWAYS SEE THINGS
            FROM MY POINT OF VIEW.

POT-SHOTS NO. 246

I HAVE SO MANY
WONDERFUL QUALITIES,

IT'S EASY TO OVERLOOK
MY FEW DISGUSTING HABITS.

Ashleigh Brilliant

1980, p. 157). I want to make sure you know about these triumphs because so far the number of people who have ever told me they had noticed either of them amounts to three, one of whom was my mother.

Another kind of success is that of being officially translated into other languages. But there are some difficulties here. Should I, for example, insist that the foreign versions of my works also be limited to seventeen words? That would in a way be unfair, because many other languages seem to need more words than English to say the same thing. Perhaps I should allow the Germans an extra word. This could be specified in the contract, giving it (as I hallucinate) the grandeur of an international treaty. I can see the headlines: *ASHLEIGH BRILLIANT GRANTS 18TH WORD TO GERMANY — CRISIS AVERTED — HUGE CROWDS GATHER TO GIVE THANKS.*

Show Us a Sign

But there is something else I am more and more frequently beseeched to grant, to the point where it has become for me the most questionable symbol of pseudo-success: my autograph. Setting aside possible historical value, there is nobody in the world whose signature I personally would go out of my way to request, unless it were attached to a highly laudatory testimonial, or to some pleasantly meaningful personal document, such as a check. And the whole thing has in recent times become something of a racket, with the lure of an author's autograph being used to sell his books.

But it obviously does give some people real pleasure to have this evidence that I actually exist. Nevertheless, it can become very onerous when a great many people all demand such proof; and I have lately been forced to consider three possible alternatives: (1) refuse (like the British Royal Family) to give autographs at all; (2) start making a charge for them; (3) authorize somebody else to autograph my books for me. The first alternative, however, seemed too extreme, and the second too risky (I might discover just how little I am really worth). The third idea seemed rather a good one to me, but my wife, whom I nominated for the role, said it would make her feel like a forger.

15

I have therefore taken it upon myself to give you a facsimile autograph which I am hoping may satisfy at least some of your (perfectly understandable) craving to have my individual blessing bestowed upon you. I hope also that it will start a trend to remove some of the mystique which for some reason distinguishes authors from other equally meritorious workers. After all, why don't you ask the bus-driver to autograph your ticket, or the dentist to autograph your teeth?

What Is All This?

As a trained scholar, I have more than a casual interest in knowing what cultural category to put myself in. But such a question is not easy to answer when I am deliberately trying to do something different from what has ever been done before. In any existing classification I am bound to feel at least slightly uncomfortable.

As you will see on the reverse of the title page of this book, the U.S. Library of Congress (no doubt after much serious study and debate), has decided that my works should be classified primarily as "Epigrams." My Random House Dictionary turns that word into something of a compliment: "Any witty, ingenious, or pointed saying, tersely expressed." (Do I thank the Library of Congress, or do I thank Random House?) Well, if I am indeed a professional epigrammatist (yes, there is such a word) I am a member of a very rare breed. But even if you include part-time practitioners, you will find that the epigrams other people have been writing are nothing like mine. Theirs may ramble on for sentences or even for paragraphs; mine must not go beyond seventeen words. Theirs may indulge in rhyme, rhythm, puns, or references to current events; mine are forbidden to enter those territories. Mine have had everything boiled out of them except the meaning and the fun. With Brilliant Thoughts, you say good-bye to word games and enter the realm of pure (or impure) ideas.

I am also possibly the first writer of epigrams to adopt what might be called the "wandering I" — to write frequently in the first person without ever identifying the speaker. Of course, no identification is really necessary. If the words mean anything to you at all, you know who is saying them, or else it doesn't matter.

Another distinguishing feature of these works is of course the fact that they are illustrated by the author. Even the great La Rochefoucauld, who seems to have come as close as anybody to being my illustrious predecessor, apparently never thought of bringing out an illustrated edition of his *Maximes*, let alone of doing the art himself. I have worked very hard on illustrating mine, but will admit that some of my attempts are more successful than others. That is one reason why, in addition to reading them to yourself and enjoying the pictures, I urge you to try reading these Thoughts aloud to others, who may get even more pleasure out of forming their own mental pictures.

But some great works are even greater if not analyzed too closely; and, despite my own felt need to understand just what I am doing, that may be true — who knows? — of what you find on the following pages. I have no objection, however, to the institution of Ashleigh Brilliant study groups and research projects, or even the formation of Ashleigh Brilliant Fan Clubs, just so long as they require nothing more from me than permission to appreciate. But it must be obvious to you by now that, if you really want to appreciate me, you should get your application in soon.

Life Sentences

You and I have at least one thing in common — a thing called life. At the time I write this, yours may not yet even have begun. At the time you read this, mine may already be long past. Or, just possibly, by one of those incredibly dramatic coincidences, we may both actually be living at the same time. But, whatever the chronology, this common experience of what seems to be a very remarkable phenomenon somehow links us, and certainly provides us with superb material for communication.

Just exactly what life is has not yet been satisfactorily explained to me, and perhaps you too are still in some doubt. But we all know that it concerns having something called a body, which somehow finds itself in something called a world. The whole thing may very well be somebody's mistake, although, without more information, it's hard to know just where to place the blame. It may also be an illusion, a joke, a lesson, a special treat, a test, or (perhaps more likely) something for which the right words haven't yet been invented.

But fortunately there *are* words which enable us to have our say about how it feels to be in this odd condition; and I hereby offer you a bunch, gathered in the course of many curious journeys to distant corners of my mind.

Ashleigh Brilliant

Any life
that begins
with a birth
and ends with
a death
must inevitably
seem
rather strange.

© ASHLEIGH BRILLIANT

© ASHLEIGH BRILLIANT 1981.

POT-SHOTS NO. 2166.

THE TASK
I'VE BEEN GIVEN
SEEMS ABSURD:

TO WAIT HERE
ON EARTH
UNTIL I
NO LONGER EXIST.

Ashleigh Brilliant

IF MY LIFE
HAD BEEN
EASIER TO LIVE,

I MIGHT ALREADY
HAVE FINISHED
LIVING IT.

© ASHLEIGH BRILLIANT 1981.

WHY DO I SO OFTEN DESIRE THE BEST?

Ashleigh Brilliant

And why do I so seldom get it?

WHAT IS THIS "REAL LIFE" I KEEP HEARING ABOUT?

Ashleigh Brilliant

21

THE LONGE
I LIVE,

THE LESS CHANC
I'LL EVER RECOVI
FROM WHAT LIFE
KEE
DOI
TO
M

IT
WOULD HELP
IN ATTACKING
MY PROBLEMS,

IF I KNEW
THE EXACT
LOCATION
OF THEIR
WEAKEST POINT.

I play
small roles
in many
people's lives,
but in my own
I play
a principal part.

© ASHLEIGH BRILLIANT 1981.

BRILLIANT ENTERPRISES 1972

WE GET
SOME KIND
OF WEATHER HERE
NEARLY EVERY DAY.

Ashleigh Brilliant

© BRILLIANT ENTERPRISES 1976

I'LL BE GLAD WHEN IT'S ALL OVER, AND I CAN TAKE MY SMILE OFF.

Ashleigh Brilliant

ASHLEIGH BRILLIANT 1981.

LIFE
IS NOT NECESSARILY
SOMETHING I WOULD
RECOMMEND
TO EVERYBODY.

Ashleigh Brilliant

I KNOW A WAY TO MAKE PLEASURE LAST LONGER:

I PRETEND THAT IT'S PAIN.

Ashleigh Brilliant

Ashleigh Brilliant

It sometimes takes longer than one lifetime between knowing what you ought to do and doing it.

POT-SHOTS NO. 2279.

Ashleigh Brilliant

SOMETIMES IT SEEMS MY WHOLE LIFE IS A SURPRISE PARTY.

POT-SHOTS NO. 920.

Ashleigh Brilliant

WE REALLY OUGHT TO DO SOMETHING ABOUT DEATH—

Do you have any suggestions?

Life is a
process
of losing
our
illusions,

until
finally,
we lose
the illusion
that we're
alive.

Ashleigh Brilliant

I TRY TO TAKE LIFE AS IT COMES,

AND JUST HOPE IT KEEPS COMING.

Ashleigh Brilliant

I could do
great things,

*Ashleigh
Brilliant*

IF I WEREN'T SO BUSY
DOING LITTLE THINGS.

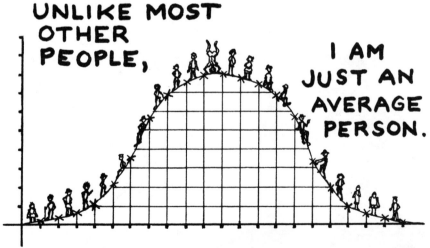

UNLIKE MOST
OTHER
PEOPLE,

I AM
JUST AN
AVERAGE
PERSON.

Ashleigh Brilliant

LIFE IS THE ONLY GAME

IN WHICH
THE OBJECT
OF THE GAME

Ashleigh Brilliant

IS TO
LEARN
THE
RULES.

© ASHLEIGH BRILLIANT 1979

© ASHLEIGH BRILLIANT 1981.

SOME OF THE THINGS
I HAVE TO DO
ARE
MORE EASILY
DONE

IF I'M NOT
FULLY
CONSCIOUS.

Ashleigh Brilliant

MOST OF MY PROBLEMS EITHER HAVE NO ANSWER

OR ELSE
THE ANSWER
IS WORSE THAN
THE PROBLEM.

Ashleigh Brilliant

IF YOU LIKE PUZZLES,

You should
find Life
very
enjoyable.

Ashleigh Brilliant

EVERY TIME I TRY TO TAKE OUT A NEW LEASE ON LIFE,

THE
LANDLORD
RAISES
THE RENT.

gh Brilliant

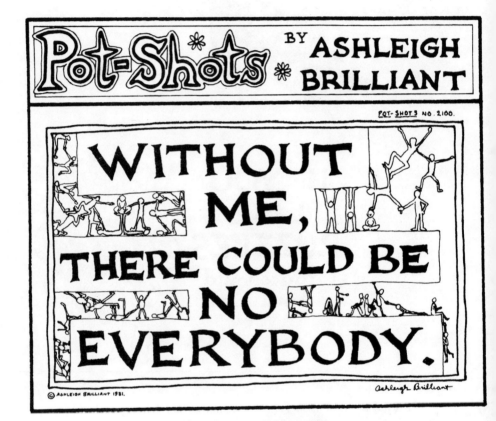

Self Conscious

Everybody is entitled to a self. But some of us have several, while others are hard-pressed to make contact with even one. And even when contact has been established, the process of identification can be lengthy and tedious. In fact, vast amounts of time and money are spent by the members of that rather exclusive club called Modern Society trying to prove to ourselves and each other exactly who we are. We have passports, licenses, identity badges, credit cards, birth certificates, and innumerable other documents, to say nothing of fingerprints, voiceprints, and perhaps eventually brain-prints and soulprints. Armed with these proofs, we march through life, demonstrating over and over again to a skeptical world that we are indeed the person whom we claim — and often believe ourselves — to be, and distinguishable from all others.

But mere differentiation is not enough. A name, a face, and a few statistics — even your own — need to be clothed with some additional data before any self-respecting self can begin to emerge from the great mass of nobodies which confronts us. This is a chore we usually assign to a somewhat befuddled and rather-too-anxious-to-please servant called Memory. We keep him busy throughout our lives, constantly bringing out revised, updated, and carefully censored editions of our self-story, illustrated with our self-picture. In the end, however, he loyally jumps into the grave with us, and all we leave behind of self is one final futile identity document — a few words and numbers carved on a stone.

GIVE ME STRENGTH TO FACE MY WEAK-NESSES.

Ashleigh Brilliant

I AM NOT DANGEROUS TO ANYBODY

EXCEPT, POSSIBLY,
IN SOME WAYS,
TO MYSELF,

© ASHLEIGH BRILLIANT 1981.

Ashleigh Brilliant

Ashleigh Brilliant

I THINK
MY LIFE IS
TRYING TO
TELL ME
SOMETHING,

BUT
I DON'T
HAVE TIME
TO LISTEN.

© BRILLIANT ENTERPRISES 1974

EVEN WHEN I'M HAPPY AND SUCCESSFUL,

Ashleigh Brilliant

LIFE STILL GOES ON.

© ASHLEIGH BRILLIANT 1981.

© ASHLEIGH BRILLIANT 1981.

I'M AS INTERESTED AS ANYBODY ELSE IN ALL THE THINGS NO DECENT PERSON WOULD BE INTERESTED I

Ashleigh Brilliant

THE THINGS I FEAR MAY ALL BE IMAGINARY

SO, WHAT I FEAR MOST IS MY IMAGINATION.

Ashleigh Brilliant

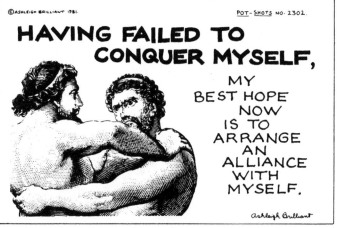

HAVING FAILED TO CONQUER MYSELF,

MY BEST HOPE NOW IS TO ARRANGE AN ALLIANCE WITH MYSELF.

Ashleigh Brilliant

The more I learn about myself,

The more I become a different self.

Ashleigh Brilliant

35

SOMETIMES
I FEEL
OUT
OF
TOUCH

WITH
MANY
THINGS
THAT ARE
HAPPENING
INSIDE
ME.

© ASHLEIGH BRILLIANT 1981.

Ashleigh
Brilliant

POT-SHOTS NO. 2325.

THE KIND OF
DISCIPLINE
I MOST
RESENT

IS
THE KIND
I IMPOSE
ON
MYSELF.

© ASHLEIGH BRILLIANT 1981.

Ashleigh
Brilliant

LET'S MEET IN PERSON:

WHAT
BETTER
WAY
CAN
THERE BE
TO COME
CLOSER TO
EACH OTHER?

Ashleigh Brilliant

Ashleigh Brilliant

HOW
COULD THERE
EVER POSSIBLY
BE ANY
CONFLICT
BETWEEN
MY
PRIVATE INTERESTS
AND
THE PUBLIC GOOD?

THIS IS SERIOUS:

SOME THINGS
SUPPOSED TO LAST
THE REST OF
MY LIFE
ARE ALREADY
WEARING OUT.

Ashleigh Brilliant

ALEIGH BRILLIANT 1981.

I'D BETTER
START BACK ~

MY EMPTY ROOM
WILL BE
GETTING
LONELY.

Ashleigh Brilliant

POT- SHOTS No. 2080.

I HOPE
I CAN
SETTLE

MY
INTERNAL
CONFLICTS

WITHOUT
BLOODSHED.

Ashleigh
Brilliant

©ASHLEIGH BRILLIANT 1981.

THERE IS
A WHOLE WORLD
WHICH
I ALONE RULE,

BUT
IT ENDS
AT MY
FINGERTIPS.

©ASHLEIGH BRILLIANT 1981.

Ashleigh Brilliant

TO WHOM SHOULD I GO FOR SOME SELF-HELP?

I'm still waiting for some public reaction to my arrival on earth.

Ashleigh
Brilliant

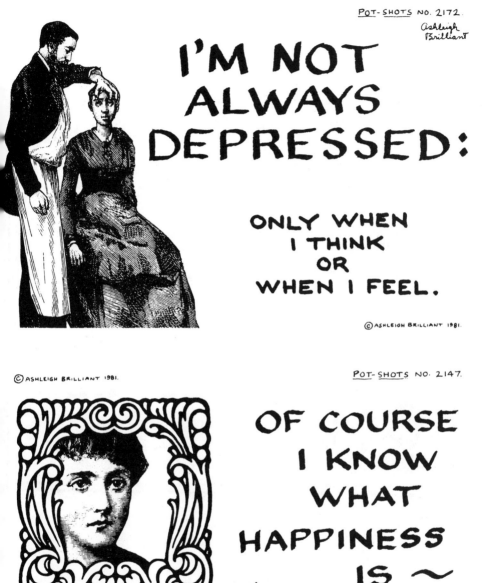

Ashleigh
Brilliant

I'M NOT ALWAYS DEPRESSED:

ONLY WHEN
I THINK
OR
WHEN I FEEL.

© ASHLEIGH BRILLIANT 1981.

© ASHLEIGH BRILLIANT 1981.

OF COURSE
I KNOW
WHAT
HAPPINESS
IS ~

Ashleigh
Brilliant

I'VE SEEN MANY PICTURES OF IT.

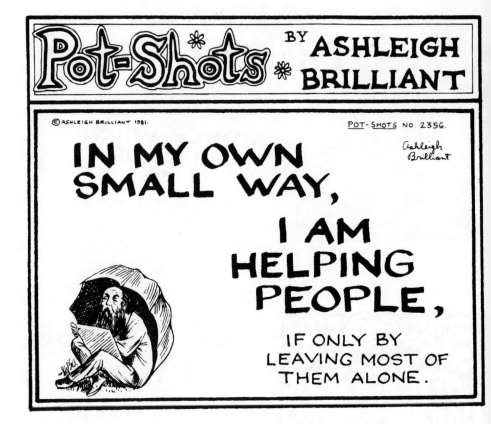

Pot-Shots BY ASHLEIGH BRILLIANT

© ASHLEIGH BRILLIANT 1981.

POT-SHOTS NO. 2356.

Ashleigh
Brilliant

IN MY OWN
SMALL WAY,

I AM
HELPING
PEOPLE,

IF ONLY BY
LEAVING MOST OF
THEM ALONE.

Social It Be

Incredible as it sometimes seems, you and I are not the only people in the world. And what to do about all those Others can occasionally be a serious social problem. The worst of it is that they desperately want our attention. If you just try to ignore them, they will shut off your water or your lights, or even your love.

Living on the same planet with them can be a hazardous and bothersome business. They weave sticky nets of obligations; they put up dreary walls of prohibitions; they become obsessed with mad and dangerous desires to educate, to cultivate, to medicate.

But even among such strange creatures, it is still possible to find allies. Some actually lie in ambush waiting sometimes for many years, just for a chance suddenly to spring out and befriend you. Others you may rarely see in person, since they themselves are often being held captive in remote families, schools and occupations. But somehow they manage to smuggle out little messages which, in one way or another, like many of those on these pages, say, "Secretly, I'm on your side."

COLD COMFORT:

SOME OF THE WORST THINGS I'VE DONE HAVE PROBABLY BEEN FORGOTTEN BY EVERYBODY,

EXCEPT ME.

Ashleigh Brilliant

NOBODY HAS EVER LOVED ME

THE WAY I REALLY THINK

EVERYBODY SHOULD LOVE ME.

Ashleigh Brilliant

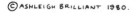

OPINIONS ARE DIVIDED
AS TO WHETHER OR NOT THERE IS
REAL UNANIMITY
IN OUR ORGANIZATION.

POT-SHOTS NO. 2174

POT-SHOTS NO 2257

IF YOU WANT
TO START
AT THE TOP
OF YOUR
PROFESSION,

INVENT
YOUR OWN
PROFESSION.

© ASHLEIGH BRILLIANT 1981.

POT-SHOTS NO. 2263.

NOW THAT
WE'VE REACHED
AGREEMENT,

ALL WE NEED
IS TO GET
EVERYBODY
ELSE
TO AGREE
WITH US.

I HAVE
TRAVELLED WIDELY
AND HAVE
LEARNED TO
COUGH AND SNEEZE
IN MANY DIFFERENT LANGUAGES

© ASHLEIGH BRILLIANT 1978

© ASHLEIGH BRILLIANT 1981.

POT-SHOTS NO. 2246.

WHEN SEEN
FROM
THIS DISTANCE,

Your problems
are somehow
much smaller
than mine.

Ashleigh
Brilliant

© ASHLEIGH BRILLIANT 1981

POT- SHOTS NO. 205

WHAT, YOU TOO!

I THOUGHT
I WAS
THE ONLY ONE
WITH THOUGHT.
AND FEELINGS

Ashleigh Brillia

POT-SHOTS NO. 988.

E KIND TO TEACHERS

HOSE WHO
DON'T
DESERVE
YOUR
RESPECT

MAY
AT LEAST
DESERVE
YOUR
PITY.

Ashleigh
Brilliant

©ASHLEIGH BRILLIANT 1981. POT-SHOTS NO. 2354.

THERE IS MADNESS
ALL ABOUT ~

Ashleigh
Brilliant

SHALL WE
FIGHT IT,
OR JOIN IN?

GH BRILLIANT 1981. POT-SHOTS NO. 2116.

Ashleigh
Brilliant

I WOULD VOICE
MORE COMPLAINTS

IF I WEREN'T
SO AFRAID
OF THE
REMEDIES
PEOPLE
MIGHT SUGGEST.

NO MATTER HOW MUCH THE WORLD CHANGES,

BUYERS AND SELLERS WILL ALWAYS NEED EACH OTHER.

Ashleigh Brilliant

Ashleigh Brilliant

PLEASE BE PATIENT~

AT THE MOMENT I'M TOO ANGRY TO TELL YOU HOW ANGRY I AM.

DO WHAT YOU KNOW IS RIGHT, BUT TRY NOT TO GET CAUGHT.

ashleigh Brilliant

HOW MUCH OF THE INTOLERABLE SHOULD I TOLERATE, SIMPLY IN ORDER TO BE POLITE?

Ashleigh Brilliant

"TEARS WON'T
BRING HER BACK"?
~ How kind
of you
to enlighten me
on that point!

Ashleigh Brilliant

I AM NOT
UPSET,

Ashleigh
Brilliant

AND WILL
CONTINUE TO DENY
HOW UPSET I AM
UNTIL I CALM DOWN.

PLEASE
CONSIDER
THE
FEELINGS
OF OTHERS ~

ESPECIALLY
OF THOSE
WHO WOULD NEVER
TELL YOU
HOW
THEY FEEL.

Ashleigh
Brilliant

50

I WAS
EDUCATED ONCE,

AND
IT TOOK ME
YEARS
TO GET OVER IT.

I WISH
THE QUALITY
OF YOUR
PRODUCT
WERE
AS GOOD AS
THE QUALITY OF
YOUR
ADVERTISING.

Ashleigh Brilliant

IF ONLY
THE PEOPLE
I LIKE

ALL
LIKED
EACH OTHER!

Ashleigh
Brilliant

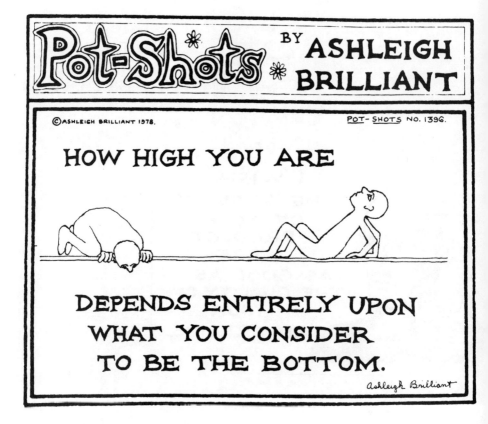

The Wise Have It

If you have a valid thinking license, some remarkable excursions are always available. Much mental territory is surprisingly seldom visited, and vast areas remain virtually unexplored. The problem is, how to bring back what you find.

I am always being asked, "Where do you get your ideas?" But, when I investigate, I usually find that the people who ask this question have just as many ideas as I do. What they really want to know is, "How do you get your ideas into useable form?" For that, I admit I have a secret technique; but, being in a generous mood, I'm willing to share it with you. It involves the use of two special devices I happen to possess, which, (although now somewhat antiquated), enable me to "freeze" ideas as they occur, and then process them later at my leisure. These wonderful instruments are known as pen and paper. Almost magically, they transform fleeting, invisible thoughts into solid, stable words. I try never to go anywhere without them, and strongly recommend them for preservation and polishing of your own ideas. But be sure that both they and you are in good working order. Too much thinking should never be done on an empty pen, or on a full piece of paper.

THERE'S
A WONDERFUL
METHOD OF
RELIEVING
FATIGUE
CAUSED BY
OVER-WORK:

IT'S CALLED
"REST".

*Ashleigh
Brilliant*

IF YOUR LIFE'S REALLY FULL,

NOTHING
YOU
EVER LOSE
WILL MAKE YOU
VERY
UNHAPPY
FOR VERY LONG.

*Ashleigh
Brilliant*

THERE'S BEEN SO MUCH CONCERN ABOUT WHAT MIGHT HAPPEN

THAT WHAT'S ACTUALLY HAPPENING HAS PASSED ALMOST UNNOTICED.

Ashleigh Brilliant

MY STRATEGY

IS, WHENEVER POSSIBLE TO KEEP OUT OF THE ARENA.

Ashleigh Brilliant

CLING TO YOUR INSECURITY!

Ashleigh
Brilliant

— IN THIS
WORLD,
IT'S THE
ONLY THING
YOU CAN
ALWAYS
BE SURE OF.

©ASHLEIGH BRILLIANT 1980.

©ASHLEIGH BRILLIANT 1979.

I KNOW SO LITTLE
THAT IT ASTONISHES ME

HOW MANY
PEOPLE
KNOW
EVEN LESS.

Ashleigh
Brilliant

MAINTAIN HIGH STANDARDS!

Ashleigh
Brilliant

REMEMBER:

CIVILIZATION
CAN SURVIVE
ONLY IF
AT LEAST SOME OF US
REMAIN CIVILIZED.

© ASHLEIGH BRILLIANT 1975.

© BRILLIANT ENTERPRISES 1975.   POT-SHOTS NO. 875.

ACCORDING TO
LATEST OFFICIAL
FIGURES,
43% OF ALL STATISTICS
ARE
TOTALLY
WORTHLESS.

Ashleigh
Brilliant

POT-SHOTS NO. 2082.

MY
COMPUTER
MUST BE
BROKEN ~

WHENEVER
I ASK
WRONG QUESTION,
IT GIVES
A WRONG ANSWER.

ASHLEIGH BRILLIANT 1981.

Ashleigh Brilliant

57

POT-SHOTS NO. 2240.

© ASHLEIGH BRILLIANT 1981.

KEEP CLIMBING UPWARDS!

YOU MAY NEVER REACH THE TOP,

BUT IT'S DEFINITELY IN THAT DIRECTION.

Ashleigh Brilliant

The reason why most living people are careful is that those who weren't are no longer living.

Ashleigh
Brilliant

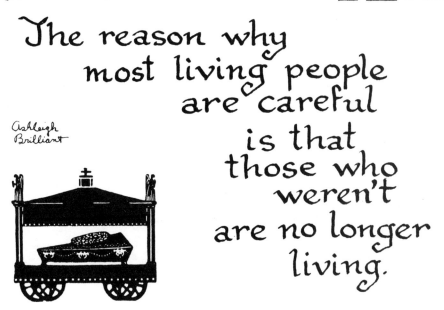

Ashleigh
Brilliant

HAVING LIVED THROUGH SOME BAD TIMES, I'M LIVING PROOF THAT SOME BAD TIMES CAN BE LIVED THROUGH.

Ashleigh Brilliant

HURRY!

DO
WHAT GOOD
YOU CAN
IN THE WORLD,
BEFORE
SOMEBODY ELSE
DOES IT ALL.

© ASHLEIGH BRILLIANT 1981.

© ASHLEIGH BRILLIANT 1981.

YOU ARE
NOT ALONE

IN YOUR
LONELINESS.

Ashleigh Brilliant

IF
YOU HIDE
YOUR
REAL FEELINGS
FOR
LONG ENOUGH,
YOU MAY
EVENTUALLY
FORGET
WHAT THEY ARE.

Ashleigh Brilliant

TRYING
TO PROVE
I COULD DO IT
AT LEAST
PROVED
ONE
THING:

THAT I
COULDN'T
DO IT.

TRY
TO BE
AS GOOD
AS YOU CAN,

WITHOUT
AROUSING JEALOUSY
OR SUSPICION.

Ashleigh Brilliant

WOULD ALL THE GOOD THINGS THAT WILL HAPPEN EVENTUALLY PLEASE TRY TO HAPPEN WHILE I'M STILL ALIVE.

Ashleigh Brilliant

IF YOU SUSPECT EVERYTHING,

YOU ARE WASTING MANY SUSPICIONS ON INNOCENT THINGS.

Ashleigh Brilliant

Ashleigh Brilliant

SOME PEOPLE KNOW HOW TO GET ON TOP OF THEIR BURDENS,

AND TURN THEM INTO PLATFORMS.

Play as You Go

Some parts of this unusual career of mine are more pleasant than others. One of the most agreeable is being free to play with words and ideas. I have only two real censors: myself and you. But those are the very same two people whom I most want to please.

I have my own ideas about good taste. I try not to offend anybody unintentionally, contriving, in any case, whenever possible, to leave my intentions wrapped in some beneficial doubt. Bear in mind that these messages began as postcards, each card giving every prospective purchaser the option of applying it in all honesty to herself or himself, sending it on, with varying degrees of spite or delight, to some other known person for whom it was obviously intended, or perhaps sighing with relief at finding it totally inapplicable to any imaginable personal situation.

Another pleasure the work has given me lies in finding inspiration for these valuable utterances in whatever I experience, wherever I go. Thus I am actually able to make a living out of my own life. This of course is to some extent true of most creative artists. The difference in my case is that, instead of having to fit whatever is on my mind into my novel or concerto, I can completely dispose of it in a self-contained ready-to-publish work of seventeen words or less, and be free to go on to something else.

An added bonus is that, if I have done my work well, that tiny literary composition, while remaining my legal property, will take on a life of its own and go through endless reproductions and reincarnations, perhaps (unlike most novels and concertos) finding its way onto your bedroom wall as a poster, your lips as a cocktail napkin, or your torso as a T-shirt. The works of few authors indeed have been able to enjoy so pleasantly intimate a relationship with their public.

HAVE PATIENCE:

ROME WAS NOT DESTROYED IN A DAY.

Ashleigh
Brilliant

I TOO HAVE KNOWN JOY AND SADNESS

Ashleigh
Brilliant

AND, ON THE WHOLE, I PREFER JOY.

POT-SHOTS NO. 1145.

THE SHOW MUST GO ON

BUT
I DON'T HAVE TO
STAY AND WATCH!

Ashleigh Brilliant

     POT-SHOTS NO. 216

Just when I nearly had the answer, I forgot the question.

Ashleigh Brilliant

SOMETIMES REALITY PRESSES DOWN ON ME,

BUT SOMETIMES I FIND MYSELF FLOATING ON TOP OF IT.

Ashleigh Brilliant

Ashleigh Brilliant

ALL THE CUSTOMS OFFICIALS ARE ON STRIKE ~

TRAVELLERS WILL HAVE TO INSPECT THEIR OWN BAGGAGE.

WHO'S IN COMMAND
OF THIS BED

Ashleigh Brilliant

POT-SHOTS NO. 2294.

**I'D
HAPPILY
SPEND
MY WHOLE
LIFE
TRAVELLING,**

IF I COULD
HAVE
ANOTHER
LIFE
TO SPEND
AT HOME.

*Ashleigh
Brilliant* © ASHLEIGH BRILLIANT 1981.

POT-SHOTS NO. 2360.

**THE DIFFERENCE
BETWEEN
PLAY-ACTING
AND REAL LIFE
IS THAT,
IN REAL LIFE,
IT'S
ALWAYS
OPENING
NIGHT.**

© ASHLEIGH BRILLIANT 1981.

Ashleigh Brilliant

© ASHLEIGH BRILLIANT 1981.

POT-SHOTS NO 2242.

**Why should I
be sensible,**

if it
prevents me
from being
happy?

*Ashleigh
Brilliant*

POT-SHOTS NO. 2311.

I'LL NEVER FORGET MY AMNESIA.

© ASHLEIGH BRILLIANT 1981.

Ashleigh Brilliant

Ashleigh
Brilliant

HAVE ARMS ~ WILL HUG.

Ashleigh Brilliant © BRILLIANT ENTERPRISES 1973

I'M UNREADY WHEN YOU ARE.

Ashleigh
Brilliant

ONE REASON
I WORK SO HARD
IS TO AFFORD
A BIG RANSOM
IF I'M
KIDNAPPED.

HOW MANY JOURNEYS MUST ONE MAKE IN ORDER TO QUALIFY AS A PROFESSIONAL PASSENGER?

Ashleigh Brilliant

BE CAREFUL WITH WATER

IT'S FULL OF HYDROGEN AND OXYGEN.

Ashleigh Brilliant

LEIGH BRILLIANT 1981.

Sometimes
I enjoy my life so much,

I just wish
it would
go on and on.

ashleigh
Brilliant

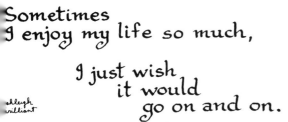

© ASHLEIGH BRILLIANT 1981.   POT- SHOTS NO. 2135.

EVEN IF YOU'RE NOT ENJOYING THE FLIGHT,

IT'S FUTILE THREATENING TO GET OUT AND WALK.

Ashleigh
Brilliant

LEIGH BRILLIANT 1981.   POT- SHOTS NO. 2108.

Ashleigh
Brilliant

N RESPONSE
TO
VERWHELMING
DEMAND,

TONIGHT'S
RFORMANCE
HAS BEEN
ANCELLED.

I SMELL AIR ON YOUR BREATH:

POT-SHOTS NO. 2077.

HAVE YOU BEEN BREATHING AGAIN?

© ASHLEIGH BRILLIANT 1981.

Ashleigh Brilliant

© ASHLEIGH BRILLIANT 1981·

POT-SHOTS NO. 2313.

I'M SO GLAD YOU TOLD ME WHAT I DIDN'T WANT TO HEAR.

Ashleigh Brilliant

POT-SHOTS NO 2032

TO BE SURE OF WINNING, INVENT YOUR OWN GAME,

AND NEVER TELL ANY OTHER PLAYER THE RULES

© ASHLEIGH BRILLIANT 1980.

Ashleigh Brilliant

THE EARTH IS A GEOLOGIST'S PARADISE.

Ashleigh Brilliant

HELP! I'M IN DESPERATE NEED OF SOME

OVERWHELMING PLEASURE.

Ashleigh Brilliant

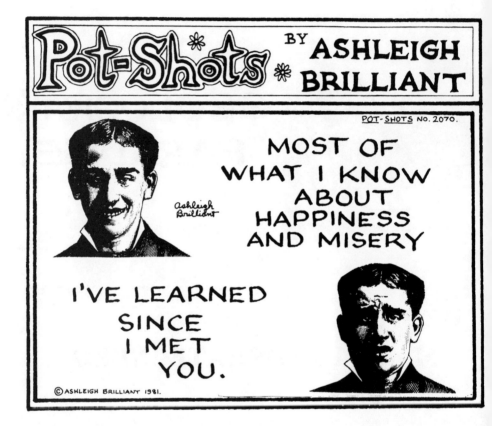

What's the Us?

I have never been very comfortable with the platitude that "two's company, three's a crowd." This may be in part because by childhood role was usually that of the excluded third person. But even from a thoroughly academic perspective it has always seemed to me that, depending on circumstances, two, or even one, could become pretty crowded. "We" are indeed a multitude, and, even within the limits of normal psychology, an amazing variety of thoughts, feelings, and even entire relationships can transpire between us. Any truly meaningful communication that takes place is therefore bound to be full of more or less subtle inconsistencies, uncertainties, and absurdities.

As a specialist in such lore, I offer you herewith some of the fruits of my research. As you will note, when simple language marches in, complex situations are often forced to withdraw in wild confusion.

YOU HAVE
THE ABILITY
TO AROUSE
VARIOUS
EMOTIONS
IN ME:

PLEASE
SELECT
CAREFULLY.

Ashleigh
Brilliant

© ASHLEIGH BRILLIANT 1981.

Do you
believe in
friendship
at
first sight?

© ASHLEIGH BRILLIANT 1981.

Ashleigh
Brilliant

WE'RE IN THIS TOGETHER,

BUT THERE'S ALWAYS

ROOM FOR ONE LESS.

Ashleigh Brilliant

FORGIVE ME

FOR ALLOWING MYSELF TO BE HURT BY YOU SO EASILY.

Ashleigh Brilliant

POT-SHOTS NO. 2232.

PLEASE DON'T
ADMIT YOUR
GUILT
BEFORE
I STOP BELIEVING
IN YOUR INNOCENCE.

Ashleigh Brilliant

© ASHLEIGH BRILLIANT 1981.

POT-SHOTS NO. 2118.

Ashleigh Brilliant

THE
PRESENT
MOMENT
IS HERE
RIGHT
NOW ~

WHY
AREN'T
YOU?

© ASHLEIGH BRILLIANT 1981.

POT-SHOTS NO. 2321.

NOBODY HAS EVER EXPLAINED THE MYSTERY

OF HOW I EXISTED BEFORE I MET YOU.

© ASHLEIGH BRILLIANT 1981.

© ASHLEIGH BRILLIANT 1979   POT-SHOTS NO. 1528.

I WANT YOUR LOVE FOR SEVERAL REASONS,

and not only
to prevent
other people
from getting it.

Ashleigh Brilliant

© ASHLEIGH BRILLIANT 1981.   POT-SHOTS NO. 218

IT'S ALWAYS GOOD TO SEE A FRIENDLY FACE ~

COULD YOU MAKE YOURS A LITTLE FRIENDLIER?

Ashleigh Brilliant

PLEASE DON'T BELIEVE EVERYTHING YOU HEAR ABOUT ME

Ashleigh Brilliant

REGARDLESS
OF
HOW TRUE
IT
MAY BE.

POT-SHOTS NO. 68

I HAPPENED TO SEE YOU PASSING THROUGH MY LIFE,

SO I THOUGHT I'D LOVE YOU.

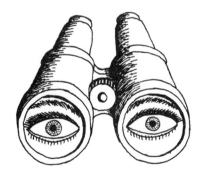

Ashleigh Brilliant

IT FRIGHTENS ME

WHEN YOU,
VERY SUDDENLY,
START TO
BEHAVE
SENSIBLY.

© ASHLEIGH BRILLIANT 1981.

Ashleigh
Brilliant

POT-SHOTS NO. 2361.

Ashleigh Brilliant

IF WE
KEEP TALKING
O EACH OTHER,

/E MAY EVENTUALLY
IND SOMETHING
VE CAN
ALK
ABOUT.

LEIGH BRILLIANT 1981.

© ASHLEIGH BRILLIANT 1981.

POT-SHOTS NO. 2341.

IS IT REALLY TRUE
THAT, ALL THE TIME
I'VE BEEN
LIVING MY LIFE,

YOU'VE BEEN
LIVING YOURS?

Ashleigh Brilliant

POT-SHOTS NO. 2079.

DON'T
TAKE IT
PERSONALLY
I NEGLECT YOU ~

Ashleigh Brilliant

LIFE
CONSTANTLY
FORCES ME
TO NEGLECT
MANY
GOOD THINGS.

LEIGH BRILLIANT 1981.

But it's only when
I misunderstand you
that I ever really
agree
with you!

Ashleigh
Brilliant

86

I KNOW
WHAT'S BEAUTIFUL
WHEN I SEE IT ~

AND
SO OFTEN
I SEE IT
IN YOU.

YOU'RE LUCKY
TO HAVE ME.

PLEASE CONTINUE
TO BE LUCKY.

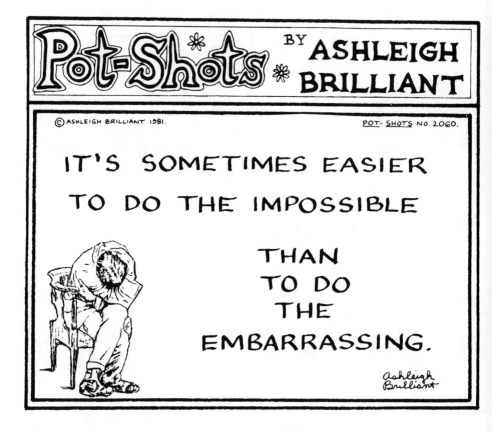

Human Writes

As citizens of that great, unruly nation called Humanity, we all accept certain occasionally wearisome duties, one of which is to maintain a complete set of attitudes and behavior-patterns. Many of these are inevitably subject to the scrutiny of our fellows, and, if we are not careful, some of the more questionable ones may even find themselves being publicly examined on postcards.

People are indeed an abundant source of my little effusions, as well as providing an ironically lucrative market for them. When I weary of exposing my own (basically lovable) shortcomings, I need look no farther than the nearest salesman (is one ever far away?) or the nearest teacher, parent, politician, or lover, for further inspiration. If the present-day begins to pall, there is always History, that inexhaustible storehouse of human error.

But there *are* good things about people, and even (on rare occasions) about being one of them. Animals and insects, for example, who have been on this earth much longer than we have, still apparently have much to learn from us in such matters as kindness and compassion, to say nothing of table manners. If forced to choose for an indefinite period between people and anything else, I would have to be in an unusually somber mood if I did not choose people (although the choice would be more difficult if "anything else" could specifically include certain varieties of chocolate).

POT-SHOTS NO. 2250.

IF WE ALL DO WHAT WE BELIEVE TO BE RIGHT,

THERE WILL ASSUREDLY BE UTTER CHAOS.

© ASHLEIGH BRILLIANT 1981.

Ashleigh Brilliant

90

IT'S HUMAN TO MAKE MISTAKES~

AND SOME OF US ARE MUCH MORE HUMAN THAN OTHERS.

Ashleigh Brilliant

MANY PEOPLE DON'T REALIZE MY IMPORTANCE IMMEDIATELY,

AND A SURPRISING NUMBER NEVER REALIZE IT AT ALL.

Ashleigh Brilliant

Ashleigh Brilliant

I HAVE NO PREJUDICES:

ALL MY IRRATIONAL HATREDS ARE BASED ON SOLID EVIDENCE.

WHEN I MOVE, I MOVE FAST ~

BUT I CAN'T REMEMBER WHEN I LAST MOVED.

Ashleigh Brilliant

THE ONLY THING
TROUBLING
MY SUPERB
SELF-CONFIDENCE

IS THE
NAGGING
POSSIBILITY
THAT YOU
MAY BE RIGHT.

TELL ME AGAIN
HOW COMPLETELY
YOU AGREE
WITH
ME.

Ashleigh Brilliant

© ASHLEIGH BRILLIANT 1981.

UNTIL I HEAR
HOW YOU ARE,

I CAN ONLY
REMEMBER

HOW YOU WERE.

Ashleigh Brilliant

94

MY OPPONENT SHOULD BE DISQUALIFIED

FOR RUNNING UNFAIRLY FAST.

WOULD YOU CARE TO VIEW THE RUINS OF MY GOOD INTENTIONS?

COMMUNICATION WITH THE DEAD IS ONLY A LITTLE MORE DIFFICULT THAN COMMUNICATION WITH SOME OF THE LIVING.

Some of
my secrets
have been
so well-kept,

I've forgotten
what they are.

Ashleigh Brilliant

MAYBE I'M WRONG,

BUT DON'T I HAVE A RIGHT TO BE WRONG?

Ashleigh Brilliant

HIS IS A CODE MESSAGE ~

THE CODE IS CALLED "LANGUAGE".

ARE YOU RECEIVING ME?

Ashleigh Brilliant

POT-SHOTS NO. 2212.

DON'T LET YOURSELF SUFFER NEEDLESSLY ~

FIND A NEED TO SUFFER.

© ASHLEIGH BRILLIANT 1981.

Ashleigh Brilliant

98

BUT I CAN'T FUNCTION WHEN I'M CALM!

Ashleigh Brilliant

I MAY ACCEPT EVERY POINT IN YOUR ARGUMENT,

BUT WILL NEVER AGREE WITH YOUR INESCAPABLE CONCLUSION.

Ashleigh Brilliant

World Serious

Despite many rumors to the contrary, there is still a world outside your door. In case the significance of this fact escapes you, let me remind you that, quite apart from anything else, we are all dependent on the world for most of our world news. That news, I must admit, is one of my own chief sources of entertainment. Where else can you find such a cast of characters, such a complicated and intriguing plot, such continuous and varied action, and such masterful suspense, with a completely new episode coming out every day? The only drawback is that sometimes the news comes a little too close to home; but even in that possibility lies part of the excitement, which no other show can provide.

It would of course be nice if, in addition to observing the world scene, one could actually do something to improve it. Yet even those who attain the highest positions of leadership often seem hard put simply to prevent things from getting any worse. Despite this, my own feeling is that ours is a better time to be alive than any previous one. Although modern technology is not entirely easy to coexist with, I am (at least in theory) generally on its side, particularly since, in so many ways, it is kind enough to help me reach you.

POT-SHOTS NO. 2285.

THE WORLD IS A VERY STRANGE COMMUNITY,

BUT IT'S THE ONLY ONE WE ALL BELONG TO.

POT-SHOTS NO. 2296.

WORK ON CONSTRUCTION OF AN IDEAL WORLD HAS BEEN TEMPORARILY HALTED,

DUE TO A SHORTAGE OF IDEALISTS.

FREEDOM
IS NOT
THE GOAL,

BUT
YOU NEED FREEDOM
BEFORE
YOU CAN DECIDE
WHAT THE GOAL IS.

© ASHLEIGH BRILLIANT 1981.

©ASHLEIGH BRILLIANT 1981.

POT-SHOTS NO. 2265.

MAKE
YOURSELF
USEFUL
TO YOUR
OPPRESSORS,

UNTIL YOU'RE
STRONG ENOUGH
TO OVERTHROW THEM.

Ashleigh Brilliant

.RIGH BRILLIANT 1981.

POT-SHOTS NO. 2076.

WILL ALL THOSE
VHO FEEL POWERLESS
TO INFLUENCE EVENTS

PLEASE SIGNIFY
BY
MAINTAINING
THEIR USUAL
SILENCE.

Ashleigh Brilliant

WHY IS THERE ALWAYS
SUCH A POWER STRUGGLE

WITHIN THE
MOVEMENT
FOR PEACE
AND
FRIENDSHIP?

Ashleigh
Brilliant

© ASHLEIGH BRILLIANT 1981.

I'M NOT YET DESPERATE ENOUGH TO DO ANYTHING ABOUT THE CONDITIONS WHICH ARE DRIVING ME TO DESPERATION.

POT-SHOTS NO. 2323

IF THINGS ARE NOT AS BAD AS THEY SEEM,

WHY DO THEY SEEM SO BAD?

© ASHLEIGH BRILLIANT 1981.

© ASHLEIGH BRILLIANT 1981.

POT-SHOTS NO. 2177.

Ashleigh Brilliant

I HAVE NOTHING DEFINITE TO APOLOGIZE FOR:

I'M JUST SORRY ABOUT EVERYTHING IN GENERAL.

WHO WILL SAVE THE WORLD

FROM ALL THE STRANGE PEOPLE

WHO THINK ONLY THEY CAN SAVE IT?

© ASHLEIGH BRILLIANT 1979.

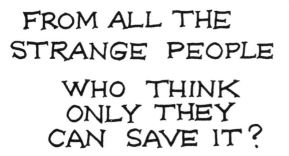

© ASHLEIGH BRILLIANT 1981.

WHY IS IT THAT THE WORLD'S MOST BEAUTIFUL

REMAINING PLACES ARE THOSE MOST DIFFICULT TO REACH?

BAD COOKING
CAN AT LEAST
BE THROWN AWAY,

Ashleigh Brilliant

BUT
BAD ARCHITECTURE
IS MUCH HARDER
TO DISPOSE OF.

© BRILLIANT ENTERPRISES 1977.

© ASHLEIGH BRILLIANT 1981.

POT-SHOTS NO. 2110.

PEOPLE WHO CAN AFFORD THE BEST

ARE NOT
NECESSARILY
OTHERWISE
WORTHY
OF IT.

Ashleigh Brilliant

POT- SHOTS NO. 2235.

Ashleigh
Brilliant

THE PUBLIC
IS ALWAYS
IN THE MAJORITY

BUT SOMEHOW
NEVER REALLY
HAS
THE
POWER.

POT- SHOTS NO. 819.

Ashleigh
Brilliant

I WANT
REVENGE

FOR ALL MY
REAL AND IMAGINED
GRIEVANCES.

THERE'S
LITTLE
IN THE
WORLD
I CAN
CHANGE,

AND, OF THAT,
VERY LITTLE
WANTS
TO BE CHANGED.

Ashleigh Brilliant

THE WHOLE WORLD IS OUR DINING-ROOM ~

Ashleigh Brilliant

BUT BE CAREFUL:

IT IS ALSO OUR GARBAGE-CAN.

TODAY'S CHILDREN ARE REQUIRED TO LEARN

Ashleigh Brilliant

WHAT MOST PEOPLE IN FORMER TIMES WERE FORBIDDEN TO KNOW.

So I Thought

The life of a professional thinker (which is what, in essence, and greatly to my own surprise, I seem to have become) is not so very different from that of anybody else. My body does most of the strange things yours does. It wears clothing, processes food, and goes through that uncanny alternation of sleeping and waking. The one major difference is that, in addition, I have been conditioned to salivate mentally whenever I am exposed to any fragment of experience capable of being rendered into a meaningful expression of seventeen words or less.

Even so, the words do not usually fall into place of their own accord, and there are always difficulties to contend with. One of these is the danger of anticipating myself. For example, just this morning I was walking past our local tennis club, and noticed a big garbage truck making its collection there. Immediately, my mental jaws began to do their work, chewing on the idea of making some clever connection between the hauling of refuse and the game of tennis. But then I suddenly realized that it was useless to pursue that plan any further. I had already (though quite inadvertently) filled that very bill many years earlier when I produced Brilliant Thought No. 10: *BEFORE WE MAKE LOVE, WOULD YOU MIND TAKING OUT THE GARBAGE?*

POT-SHOTS NO. 2287.

DO WHAT'S EASY ~

WITH ANY LUCK AT ALL, IT MAY ALSO BE WHAT'S RIGHT.

Ashleigh Brilliant

© ASHLEIGH BRILLIANT 1981.

114

What makes things
so difficult
is that
I've never been
at this point
in my life
before.

Ashleigh
Brilliant

TO BE
PERFECTLY
HONEST,

I SOMETIMES
FIND IT
VERY DIFFICULT
TO BE
PERFECTLY
HONEST.

Ashleigh
Brilliant

One way
to fill your life
is to spend it
reading about
how other people
filled theirs.

Ashleigh
Brilliant

THE
BEST THING
ABOUT MY
LACK OF
PROGRESS

IS THAT
I CAN'T
FALL BACK
VERY FAR.

Ashleigh Brilliant

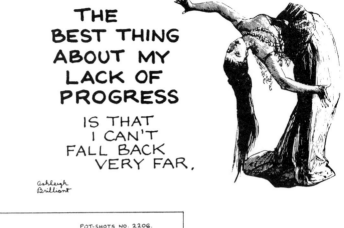

WHY IS IT THAT
MANY OF THE MOST
IMPORTANT
THINGS

Ashleigh Brilliant

ARE
ALSO
THE MOST
BORING?

WHY DO SO MANY
OF THE THINGS
I DID
YESTERDAY

Ashleigh Brilliant

ALWAYS NEED
TO BE DONE
AGAIN
TODAY?

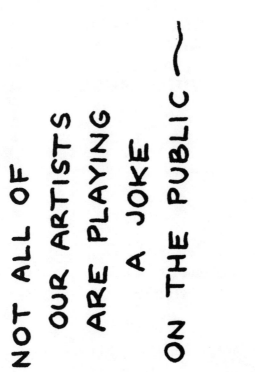

POT-SHOTS NO. 1383.

NOT ALL OF
OUR ARTISTS
ARE PLAYING
A JOKE
ON THE PUBLIC ~

SOME ARE
GENUINELY MAD.

Ashleigh Brilliant

OBVIOUSLY
THERE'S
A
DIFFERENCE
BETWEEN
BIG
AND
LITTLE,

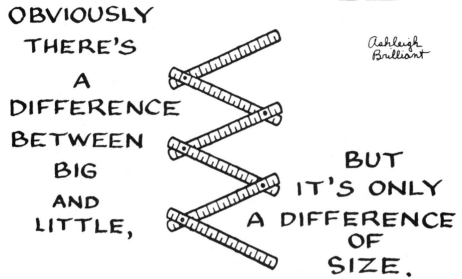

Ashleigh Brilliant

BUT
IT'S ONLY
A DIFFERENCE
OF
SIZE.

I WISH
I COULD PROVE
THAT I'M
NOT
AFRAID
OF DEATH

Ashleigh Brilliant

WITHOUT
HAVING TO
RISK MY LIFE.

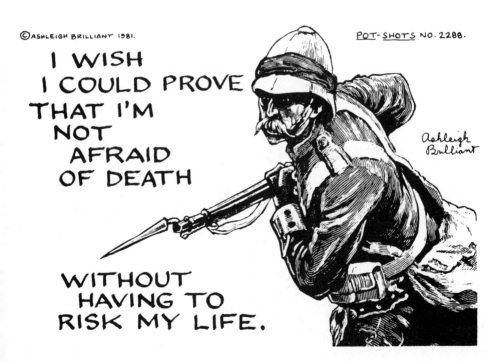

THANK GOD FOR MAKING REALITY,

AND FOR GIVING US MEANS OF ESCAPING FROM IT.

Ashleigh Brilliant

Ashleigh Brilliant

Perhaps the world's only purpose is to give me something to think about.

INTELLIGENCE is not

of much use,

unless you're

intelligent enough

o know how to use it.

RILLIANT ENTERPRISES 1974.

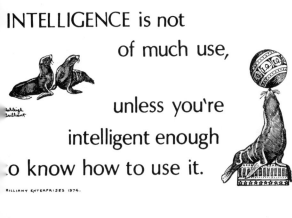

© ASHLEIGH BRILLIANT 1981.   POT-SHOTS NO. 2305.

PLEASE DON'T STEAL MY IDEAS

BEFORE I'VE PERFECTED THEM.

Ashleigh Brilliant

I'VE LOST FAITH IN MOST THINGS,

BUT STILL BELIEVE IN THE IMPORTANCE OF COMFORTABLE CLOTHING.

LEIGH BRILLIANT 1981.

POT-SHOTS NO. 2328.

MUST I
LIVE THROUGH ALL THE
DULL PARTS
OF
MY LIFE?

ISN'T THERE
A
CONDENSED
VERSION?

© ASHLEIGH BRILLIANT 1981.

Ashleigh Brilliant

I'LL GIVE UP MY BAD HABITS

AS SOON AS EQUALLY SATISFYING GOOD HABITS BECOME AVAILABLE.

© ASHLEIGH BRILLIANT 1981.

IF I ALWAYS DO TOMORROW'S WORK TODAY,

THE LAST DAY OF MY LIFE WILL BE TOTALLY FREE.

1980 Ashleigh Brilliant

Ashleigh Brilliant

Pot-Shots

BY ASHLEIGH BRILLIANT

POT-SHOTS
NO. 2247.

TOMORROW
IS
ANOTHER
DAY ~

BUT I HOPE
IT'S NOT
ANOTHER DAY
LIKE
THIS ONE.

Ashleigh
Brilliant

Forever and a Delay

For some reason, I always seem to spend much of my thinking time thinking about time. And so, apparently, do many of my readers. "How long did it take you to do this?" is a question I am very often asked. The only really honest answers are "a few hours" or "all my life."

My first paid and published piece of writing appeared in the children's section of the Washington, D.C., *Sunday Star* on January 27, 1946, when I was twelve years old. It was a 246-word story, about a knight named Gezuntite (my spelling for Gesundheit) who hears a series of screams one day, while out riding on his horse, Radish. (This, I remember, was my father's contribution, when I asked him, "What would be a funny name for a horse?") He decides that the screams are a code message, which he spends most of the story trying to decode. By the time he has found out that the message means "HELP!" his rival has rescued and carried off the maiden. For this epic I was paid one dollar.

Possibly it was from that time that I began to entertain the fantasy of someday being able to earn my living as a writer. But that dream did not even begin to come true until some 21 years later, when I started to publish and distribute my own work (a recourse which I recommend without question to all frustrated geniuses).

Since then, time has enabled me to refine my style and shorten my stories somewhat, although you will have observed that they are still much involved with Gezuntite's old problem of communication. But this great literary experiment is no doubt still in its infancy. Given a few more centuries (perhaps with occasional ten-year breaks for rest and reflection), there is no telling to what lengths (or brevities) you and I could take it.

HOW MUCH MORE OF
THE PRESENT DO WE
HAVE TO SIT THROUGH
BEFORE THE FUTURE
COMES ON?

Ashleigh
Brilliant

WHY DO OLD PEOPLE KEEP LIVING? ~

BECAUSE IT'S
ONE OF THE
HARDEST
HABITS
TO BREAK,

Ashleigh
Brilliant

THE CASE
HAS BEEN GOING ON
SO LONG
THAT I'VE FORGOTTEN
WHETHER
I'M REALLY
INNOCENT
OR GUILTY.

© ASHLEIGH BRILLIANT 1978.

© ASHLEIGH BRILLIANT 1981.

ALL I NEED TODAY

IS ENOUGH
TO GET ME
AS FAR AS
TOMORROW.

Ashleigh
Brilliant

© ASHLEIGH BRILLIANT 1981.

POT-SHOTS NO. 2353.

Ashleigh Brilliant

I WISH THERE WERE MORE TIME

FOR THE THINGS THERE'S NEVER ENOUGH TIME FOR.

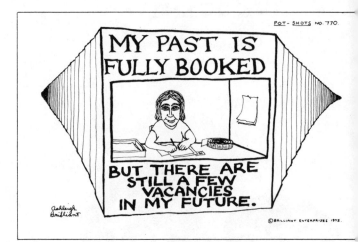

POT-SHOTS NO. 770.

MY PAST IS FULLY BOOKED

BUT THERE ARE STILL A FEW VACANCIES IN MY FUTURE.

Ashleigh Brilliant

© BRILLIANT ENTERPRISES 1975.

POT-SHOTS NO. 1583.

TODAY WILL EVENTUALLY BE A MILLION YEARS AGO,

BUT IT WILL STILL BE TODAY.

Ashleigh Brilliant

© ASHLEIGH BRILLIANT 1979.

IN THE
NEXT FEW WEEKS,
I HOPE TO DISCOVER
WHAT WILL HAPPEN
IN THE NEXT FEW WEEKS.

Ashleigh Brilliant

I BELIEVE
THERE IS
A FUTURE
SOMEWHERE
AHEAD,

EVEN THOUGH
NOT THE SLIGHTEST
EVIDENCE OF IT
EXISTS.

Ashleigh Brilliant

I FEEL TIRED,
after my
long journey
through the
past
ten
years.

Ashleigh Brilliant

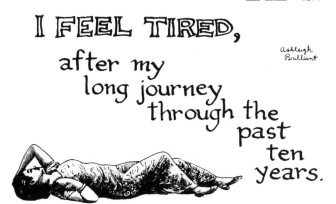

I haven't told myself that I'm getting older, because I hoped I wouldn't notice.

Ashleigh Brilliant

© ASHLEIGH BRILLIANT 1981.

IT'S VERY SAD THAT SOME PAST EVENTS WERE NOT RECORDED.

AND EVEN SADDER THAT SOME OTHERS WERE.

Ashleigh Brilliant

MORE AND MORE OF US ARE LIVING TO BE OLD,

Ashleigh Brilliant

BUT BEING OLD IS STILL EVENTUALLY FATAL.

NOTHING IS AS GOOD AS IT USED TO BE—

ESPECIALLY MY MEMORY.

Ashleigh Brilliant

Ashleigh Brilliant

The only difference between yesterday and tomorrow is: Today.

POT-SHOTS NO. 2104.

AT LEAST ONE THING ABOUT THE FUTURE IS ABSOLUTELY CERTAIN:

THAT IT HASN'T HAPPENED YET.

Ashleigh Brilliant

POT-SHOTS NO. 2224.

DYING IS A PART OF LIVING,

BUT ONLY A VERY SMALL PART.

Ashleigh Brilliant

133

POT-SHOTS NO. 2183.

Ashleigh Brilliant

Not only
don't I know
what tomorrow
will bring ~

i'm still
not exactly sure
what yesterday
brought.

© ASHLEIGH BRILLIANT 1981.

134

COULD IT BE THAT I'M ALLERGIC TO GROWING OLDER?

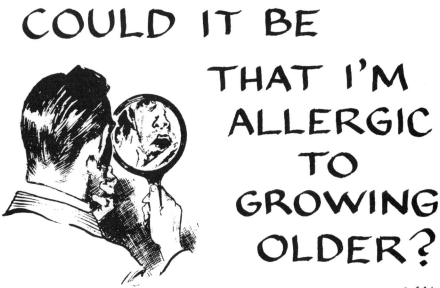

Ashleigh Brilliant

Ashleigh Brilliant

I'M GOING TO SPEND THE REST OF MY LIFE IN THE FUTURE, AND POSSIBLY EVEN LONGER.

Pot-Shots *** BY ASHLEIGH BRILLIANT

POT-SHOTS
NO. 2283.

IF I CAN'T
HAVE ACCESS
TO YOUR
HEART,

AT LEAST
LET ME HAVE
ACCESS TO
YOUR
REFRIGERATOR.

Ashleigh
Brilliant

The Kitchen Think

Of all rare and wondrous worlds, none is more engrossing than the one known as Everyday Life. It is said that those who have experienced its charms are never quite the same again. The romance of familiar figures and the same old surroundings, the glamour of habitual activities, the sheer exhilaration of plodding routine, have their parallel in no other sphere.

What better world could there be in which to begin having Brilliant Thoughts? At every point on the map of the mundane, some startling discovery lies waiting to be made. To take just one example, no Archimedes ever felt more exultant than I on the day when No. 277 flashed into my mind: *NO WONDER I'M ALL CONFUSED — ONE OF MY PARENTS WAS A MAN, THE OTHER WAS A WOMAN!* I distinctly remember that I was doing something quite ordinary at the time — so ordinary, in fact, that I have no memory at all of exactly what it was.

THERE MUST BE MORE TO LIFE THAN THIS,

OR WHAT DID I COME FOR?

Ashleigh Brilliant

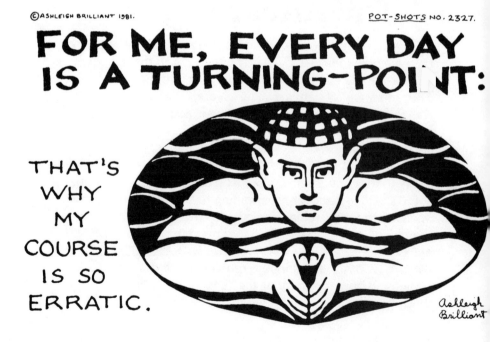

FOR ME, EVERY DAY IS A TURNING-POINT:

THAT'S WHY MY COURSE IS SO ERRATIC.

Ashleigh Brilliant

HAVE YOU BEEN DOING ANYTHING WHICH I SHOULD, OR SHOULD NOT, KNOW ABOUT?

Ashleigh Brilliant

SOME OF THE STRANGEST PEOPLE IN THE WORLD ARE MARRIED TO EACH OTHER.

Ashleigh Brilliant

POT-SHOTS NO. 2098.

EVERYTHING
MOST
PEOPLE SAY
MAKES SOME
SENSE ~

THAT'S WHY I'M
SO VERY CONFUSED.

Ashleigh Brilliant

Ashleigh
Brilliant

THE EFFORT
OF GETTING UP
IN THE MORNING

**USUALLY
EXHAUSTS ME
FOR THE
REST OF
THE DAY.**

SOMETIMES
I LONG TO
GET AWAY

FROM
TRAVELLING.

Ashleigh
Brilliant

**MANY PARENTS
PERFORM
A VALUABLE FUNCTION
SIMPLY BY GIVING
THEIR CHILDREN
SOMETHING TO
REBEL AGAINST.**

Ashleigh
Brilliant

POT-SHOTS NO. 2057.

THE
FARTHER
YOU ARE
FROM
HOME,
THE
BIGGER
AN AREA
"HOME"
BECOMES.

Ashleigh Brilliant

POT-SHOTS NO. 2331.

IS IT
YOU AND I
WHO ARE CRAZY,

OR
IS IT
EVERYBODY
ELSE?

Ashleigh Brilliant

POT-SHOTS NO. 2310.

WHERE WOULD
I BE

WITHOUT
MY
SENSE
OF
DIRECTION?

Ashleigh Brilliant

HANDLE ME WITH CARE:

I COULD BE VERY HARD TO REPLACE.

Ashleigh Brilliant

A SURPRISING NUMBER OF THE THINGS I DON'T BELIEVE ARE EVENTUALLY PROVEN TO BE UNTRUE.

Ashleigh Brilliant

ISN'T IT SAD
THAT SO MUCH HAIR
IS WANTED
WHERE IT ISN'T,
AND UNWANTED
WHERE IT IS.

Ashleigh
Brilliant

BUT IF I WERE TO
STOP AND THINK,
I MIGHT NEVER
BE ABLE TO
GET STARTED AGAIN!

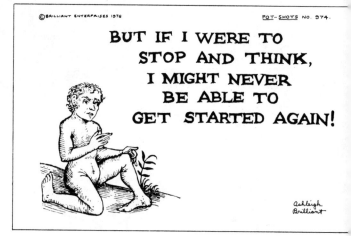

Ashleigh
Brilliant

I NEVER
BELIEVED IN
MIRACLES,

UNTIL
I WAS
BORN.

Ashleigh
Brilliant

SLAVERY AND TORTURE WERE OUTLAWED LONG AGO,

BUT, FOR SOME REASON, MARRIAGE IS STILL LEGAL.

Ashleigh Brilliant

HERE I AM AGAIN ~

BACK IN UNCERTAINTY.

Ashleigh Brilliant

© ASHLEIGH BRILLIANT 1981.

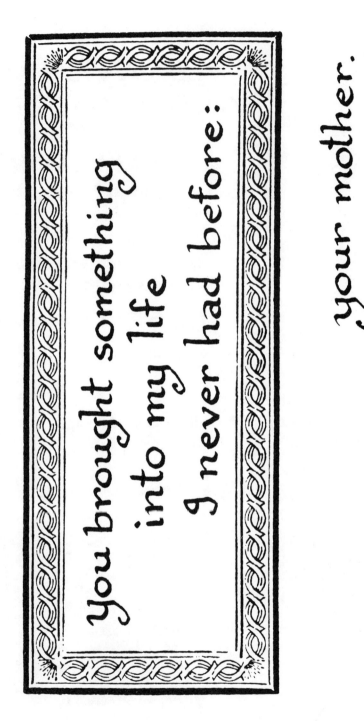

You brought something
into my life
I never had before:

your mother.

Ashleigh
Brilliant

WATCH OUT FOR CHILDREN !

SOMEDAY
THEY'LL
TAKE OVER
THE WORLD.

PREPARE FOR ETERNITY:

TIDY UP
YOUR ROOM.

Pot-Shots BY ASHLEIGH BRILLIANT

© ASHLEIGH BRILLIANT 1981.

POT-SHOTS NO. 2269.

I CAN'T IMAGINE
A LIMITED,
OR
AN UNLIMITED,
UNIVERSE ~

SO MY IMAGINATION
MUST BE
VERY LIMITED.

Ashleigh Brilliant

Just Be Cosmos

As everybody knows by now, the Universe is a big mystery. Despite mounting impatience in many quarters, and the ever-present possibility of protest demonstrations if no complete answer is forthcoming soon, not even the most advanced investigators, using the most modern equipment, have yet been able to clear it all up. Certain things, however, do appear to be more or less certain. Of these, the main one is that you can't really be certain about anything at all.

Grateful for at least that much reassurance in these troubled times, I have intermittently turned my own wavering attention to this subject, and present some of the results here, as the climax of this book. If by chance they should motivate you in any given direction, they will entirely have missed their purpose, and you should probably see your physician (or your physicist).

YES,

BUT YOU'RE TAKING THE UNIVERSE

OUT OF CONTEXT

SOMETIMES REALITY SEEMS SO NEAR,

I FEEL I COULD ALMOST TOUCH IT

THERE IS NO
MAP OF THE FUTURE,
BECAUSE NOBODY
WHO GOES THERE
EVER COMES BACK.

CHINESE:

往後怎麼樣、現在還不知道。

ashleigh Brilliant

©BRILLIANT ENTERPRISES 1972

©ASHLEIGH BRILLIANT 1981.

Ashleigh Brilliant

I'M
PERFECTLY
WILLING TO
COMPROMISE,

BUT GOD
WANTS TO HAVE
EVERYTHING
HIS OWN WAY.

POT-
SHOTS
NO. 2274.

I HAVE HEARD
THAT GOD IS
DEAD,

AND,
UNDER THE
CIRCUMSTANCES,
I'M TAKING IT VERY WELL.

Ashleigh Brilliant

© ASHLEIGH BRILLIANT 1981.

HOW WOULD THE UNIVERSE LOOK,

IF WE COULD RETURN IT TO ITS ORIGINAL CONDITION?

Ashleigh Brilliant

EVERY LITTLE THING'S MADE OF LITTLER THINGS:

ISN'T THERE ANYTHING TOO LITTLE TO BE MADE OF ANYTHING?

Ashleigh Brilliant

MANY THINGS IN THIS UNIVERSE NEED EXPLAINING ~

IF ONLY I COULD FIND SOMEBODY IN CHARGE!

THEY'VE CALCULATED THE SIZE AND AGE OF THE UNIVERSE,

BUT NOBODY HAS YET CALCULATED ITS BEAUTY.

NATURE WINS EVERY BATTLE IN THE END,

SO, WHENEVER THERE'S A CHOICE, I SIDE WITH NATURE.

GOD DOESN'T MAKE SPECIAL REPORTS TO ME ~

I JUST HAVE TO ASSUME THE UNIVERSE IS RUNNING PROPERLY.

Ashleigh Brilliant

WOULD GOD REALLY MISS ME, IF I WEREN'T HERE?

Ashleigh Brilliant

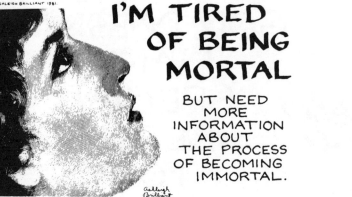

I'M TIRED
OF BEING
MORTAL

BUT NEED
MORE
INFORMATION
ABOUT
THE PROCESS
OF BECOMING
IMMORTAL.

Ashleigh
Brilliant

I KNOW
THE
UNIVERSE
IS
IMPORTANT

BUT
THERE
ARE
OTHER
THINGS
ON MY
MIND.

MANY PEOPLE
HAVE TAKEN POSITIONS
FOR AND AGAINST ATHEISM,

BUT AS YET
GOD
HAS MADE
NO COMMENT.

Ashleigh Brilliant

ELSEWHERE
HAS ALWAYS BEEN ONE OF MY FAVORITE PLACES.

Ashleigh Brilliant

Ashleigh Brilliant

ALTHOUGH I'M NOT VERY IMPORTANT, GOD, (FOR SOME REASON) HAS TAKEN THE TROUBLE TO COPYRIGHT MY FINGERPRINTS.

PROVE TO ME, IF YOU CAN, THAT, AFTER I DIE, THE WORLD WILL STILL EXIST.

Ashleigh Brilliant

LIKE YOU, I AM JUST AN ORDINARY PERSON,

LIVING IN AN EXTRAORDINARY WORLD.

Ashleigh Brilliant

FOR OBVIOUS REASONS,

ATHEISTS HAVE TO TAKE VERY GOOD CARE OF THEMSELVES.

Ashleigh Brillia

AGAIN AND AGAIN, THE EARTH INSISTS ON COMING BETWEEN ME AND THE SUN,

MAKING SOMETHING CALLED "NIGHT."

Ashleigh Brilliant

IS **LIGHT** A **WAVE**, OR A **PARTICLE**,

OR A TWINKLE IN YOUR EYE?

Ashleigh Brilliant

IT'S ALWAYS A NICE DAY IN OUTER SPACE.

Ashleigh Brilliant

Not the End

Thank you for sharing with me this precious portion of your own time on earth. I hope you have in some way found it worthwhile. If so, whatever happens, we must not let our relationship end here. There is so much more good we can do each other! If you like my books, you'll love my postcards, which make available for your individual selection a vast array of Brilliant messages, including many not appearing anywhere else. You can obtain them through a unique mail-order system of my own devising, which has been supplying many thousands of people all over the world since 1967. If the spirit moves you, send for my Catalogue, which lists the cards and other products, and comes with sample cards and an elegant order form. The current (1981) price is one U.S. dollar. Please enclose that amount, or its equivalent in your own time and currency. My address is:

Ashleigh Brilliant
117 W. Valerio Street
Santa Barbara, California 93101, U.S.A.